Aphrodisiac Cuisine

DEDICATED TO
LOUIS AND OLIVIA,
MY CHILDREN.

We are thankful to The Imperial, New
Delhi, for facilitating the photography and
forming a backdrop for this book.

ISBN: 81-7436-288-6

© Roli & Janssen BV 2003
Published in India by Roli Books
in arrangement with Roli & Janssen BV
M-75 Greater Kailash, II (Market)
New Delhi 110 048, India.
Phone: 29212271, 29212782; Fax: 29217185
E-mail: roli@vsnl.com; Website: rolibooks.com

Designed at Roli CAD Centre

Printed and bound at Singapore

Chef Bruno Cerdan

Aphrodisiac Cuisine

Photographs:
Deepak Budhraja

Lustre Press
Roli Books

Contents

Acknowledgements

A couple of years back I saw Olivia—my daughter, who was three then, create a beautiful art work with crayons. A budding artist, I thought to myself. I have also been noticing my better half, Anna add creatively pertinent touches to her business of soft furnishings. I have often admired the look of satisfaction that comes across their faces. And frankly this is what spurred me into realizing my own creative urge through a medium that I am most comfortable with. I guess, once a chef, always a chef.

Hence, when the irrepressible Pramod Kapoor approached me with the idea of doing a book on aphrodisiac cooking, I had little choice but to quietly follow my heart.

No work of any aesthetic or intellectual value gets done in isolation. There are always 'significant others' who have contributed to its genesis and creation with their ideas, stimulation or support, as the case may be.

And that is true for this venture as well. So, here I am putting on paper the Roll of Honour. I'd like to thank Pierre Jochem for his trust in my position and perspicacity and valuable support.

Also a word of gratitude to Aruna Dhir for her unstinting encouragement. Heartfelt gratitude is in order for Anna, who let me work all those extra hours and kept smiling in the face of frustration.

This is also to thank the chefs—Deepak, Mohan, Vikash, Kuldip—who helped me cook all these recipes. And Design Studio, Lotus, Carnival Homewares, and Ravissant for their beautiful products that make the pictures look luscious, edible and tantalizing as the recipes themselves.

The acknowledgement would not be complete without a mention of Louis, my seven-year-old son, who I have seen mould and model things into meaningful shapes. Thank you for being an inspiration Louis.

And last but not least many thanks to Deepak Budhraja—the immensely talented photographer, for his time, patience and most of all good humour. Bon Appetit!

Foods of Love

All it needed was a bite of the forbidden fruit and Adam and Eve were 'ready and raring to go' risking quite happily expulsion from the Garden of Eden. The apple that is supposed to keep the doctor away can be seen as the original aphrodisiac. Perhaps, that is why a hint of sin and subversion continues to cling to aphrodisiacs till present. Much later, Shakespeare was to write, 'If music be the food of love, play on . . . .' And, who can deny that music does enhance the 'many splendoured' pleasures of amour?

Foods of love have captured alike the imagination of the young and the old and broken down gender barriers. The quest for substances that can increase excitement, prolong the ecstasy during moments when bodies and minds meet is indeed eternal.

In medieval Europe *Spanish-fly* or powdered Cantharis was popular among the peasants who believed it enhanced sexual prowess. In fact, all it did was to fake the results of natural excitement. The rich had their own more expensive aids to amusement. Katherine de Medici relied upon artichokes to provide satisfaction to her husband. Stripping the sensuous vegetable, handling it delicately, and licking it after dipping in butter was a fortification as well as a prelude to more beguiling adult pastimes.

Do not confuse the culinary gems unveiled here as aphrodisiacs with crude sexual tonics sold by the quacks on the streets as guaranteed treatment for all kinds of debility or dysfunction. They belong to the realm of the erotic and the aesthetic. It is more correct to compare these offerings to a brilliant conductor who can magically transform a lifeless musical score on some sheets of paper to a tantalizing sensual symphony.

Aphrodisiacs have for long been believed to be indispensable arrows in Cupid's quiver—irresistible subtle seductions. The idea is to make the arousal as memorable as the act.

Only a philistine would think that the effect that the aphrodisiacs have is that of a placebo. You don't have to be a genius to understand that their magic works through

multi-faceted mood manipulation. Modern science has validated much-maligned conventional wisdom on the subject.

Our senses weave a delicate and complex web all the time. Smells and touch, our own experience tells us irrefutably, mingle memories with desire triggering and heightening the physical attraction we feel for another person. There is a great variety of 'mating calls' that are a prelude to the regeneration process. And, who hasn't heard of love at first sight? It is not surprising that many aphrodisiacs follow this lead.

The ingredients used often mimic the shapes—suggestively—of human genitals, like artichoke spears, or are derived from an aromatic substance like musk that is associated with the mating ritual of some animals. Eggs are included as they are obviously intrinsic to reproduction. Of course, caviar is preferable to hens' eggs! Popular imagination associates some common properties with aphrodisiac foods. Usually, such delicacies are rich, nourishing, and incorporate rare, expensive, and exotic ingredients.

In the Orient—south east Asia, China, Japan, Thailand—the tiger's penis and the bull's testicles are commonly prescribed in traditional medicine to remedy temporary or permanent sexual disability following the logic that 'like cures or replaces like'. Such cures are certainly not for the squeamish.

A touch of saffron not only improves the taste and appearance of a delicacy but also 'enriches' it, marvelously invigorating any one who imbibes it. Don't forget that saffron is obtained from the reproductive organs of the noble plant.

Pears resemble a woman's back (or is it the other way round?) and easily find a place among the pining lover-diner's wish list. Avocado pears are the fruit of the *Ahuacuatl* tree that is translated as the testicle tree. The fruit is delicious and has flesh with sensuously smooth texture. It too ranks high. Nuts and dry fruits also qualify easily. Ginger root joins as a supplement in many aphrodisiac preparations to contribute and reinforce the effect of other partners.

Aphrodite, the Geek Goddess of Love, was, we are told, born from sea foam—hence all seafood is believed to be touched with some special magic. The Aztec Indians maintained that chocolate was the nourishment of gods who knew no waning of desire or failure of performance. Interestingly, seafood is rich in iodine and phosphorus and chocolate is a rich repository of de-oxidant. These

foods if consumed in moderation are very healthy and can in fact retard aging.

In India, precious metals and gems have long been used to rejuvenate body and mind. Gold, silver, corals, and peals are consumed as *bhasma*—literally ashes. The Yunani / Arab system of medicine terms these products as *kushta*. There is an interesting mythological story that explains their power in a 'fired' form. Lord Shiva once reduced Kama, the Indian Cupid, to ashes because he had dared disturb his meditation. These ashes, we are told, are therefore charged with exceptional potency and this is what re-energizes the user.

It is well known that aphrodisiacs generate heat, mimicking the normal changes in the body when we are excited: increasing heart beats, fast breathing, etc. The idea, it seems, is to cause a rush of blood, causing the face to flush signalling lust, or a blush, indicating a shy assent. The therapy works by maybe applying an irritant or astringent intelligently so as to simulate natural excitement. Thus are dying embers often rekindled!

Aphrodisiacs do hold out hope of titillating even the most jaded palate by tempting the tired taste buds with a different taste, offering the flavour of fantasy. At the same time, many of the ingredients used have tonic properties which, it is reasonable to believe, do contribute to reinvigorate a body enfeebled due to excessive exertions in the pursuit of pleasure.

The *Kamasutra*, an ancient Indian treatise on the pleasures of the flesh, has an entire chapter devoted to edible and some externally applied substances that we are told are 'time tested' and come to the rescue of the sexually distressed.

We have come a long way since. *Vatsyayana* the author of the *Kamasutra* and Viagra, the wonder drug, are separated by a millennia but what has remained constant is our yearning for eternal youth and attempts to prolong the physical enjoyment associated with it.

In fact aphrodisiacs work subliminally—accelerating anticipation, recalling shared pleasures in times past, promising a novel encounter with ecstasy. Aphrodisiacs are akin to 'candles and whispering sweet nothings' that create an inviting ambiance for love play.

Only the vulgar minded can see them as a witch's brew or a magic potion, desperate and at times dangerous remedy for impotence or frigidity. Their role, in fact, is similar to that of a pillow book that encourages and enables lovers and would-be lovers as they share its pages to shed their inhibitions, leave behind any residual innocence and explore the joys of sex with a sense of abandon. They are like marvelous miniature paintings, blurring the borders between the carnal and the sublime. Anyway, who wants to be shackled by reason in the realm of passion?

The proof of the pudding they say is in the eating and Chef Bruno Cerdan has put an inspired performance to serve the cause of lovers. He has ably demonstrated in his labour of love that there are many options that blend the therapeutic with the artistic. No mean accomplishment this.

He has endeavored to compile a selection of the best recipes from all over the world. He brilliantly showcases how the classic culinary heritage and *avant-garde* fusion can complement each other for this purpose. The aperitifs, main courses, and desserts prepared by him promise to contribute to a fine dining experience, stimulating and satisfying at the same time. This imaginative 'aphrodisiac repast' addresses itself to the different needs of foreplay, actual lovemaking and the afterglow.

Before embarking on this sensuous sampling of irresistible temptations it is useful to recall that there are some foods that work as stimulant to inspire and prod on the sluggish; others that are soothing and tranquilizing to slow down the impatient and reassure the anxious so that their party is not prematurely pooped! Plan your menu carefully.

— Pushpesh Pant

drinks
soups and
appetizers

A glass or two of champagne can greatly enhance a romantic interlude. It relaxes and helps to stimulate the senses. Drinking champagne can be an erotic experience.

STRAWBERRY AND CHAMPAGNE 'DESIR'

Ingredients:

200 gm	Strawberries	**For the sugar syrup—boil together for 5 minutes:**
1 cup / 250 ml	Champagne	7½ tbsp / 150 gm Sugar
		²/₃ cup / 160 ml Water

Method:

1. Blend the strawberries (keeping 2 whole ones aside for garnishing) in a food processor with the champagne. Add the sugar syrup to get the required fluid consistency. Refrigerate.
2. Serve chilled in individual glasses, garnished with strawberry.

(See p. 12 **top** for picture)

MANGO AND RUM 'TEMPTATION'

Ingredients:

220 gm	Mango pulp	1 cup / 250 ml	Sugar syrup
1 cup / 250 ml	White rum	1	Cinnamon stick, 1½" piece
a pinch	Cinnamon powder	2	Star anise

Method:

1. Blend the mango pulp in a food processor at a very high speed. Add the white rum, cinnamon powder, and sugar syrup to get the required fluid consistency. Refrigerate.
2. Serve chilled, garnished with cinnamon stick and star anise.

*(See p. 12 **middle** for picture)*

KIWI AND GIN 'MI AMOR'

Ingredients:

4	Kiwis, peeled, sliced	2 tbsp / 30 ml	Crème de menthe
1 tbsp / 15 ml	Gin	1 cup / 250 ml	Sugar syrup
		2 tbsp / 40 ml	Cream

Method:

1. Keep a few slices of kiwis aside for garnishing. Blend the remaining kiwis in a food processor with gin and crème de menthe.
2. Add the sugar syrup, if required, to get the right fluid consistency. Add the cream just before serving. Garnish with a slice of kiwi.

*(See p. 12 **bottom** for picture)*

The kiwi has an elusive flavour. Some say it is reminiscent of pineapple... others say strawberry... but all agree that it has a sweet-tart flavour unlike any other fruit.

Asparagus is an exotic vegetable, the smooth shape enhances the desire. Folklore suggests that eating asparagus can cure bee stings, ease toothache and restore eyesight.

TOMATO AND ASPARAGUS SOUP

Ingredients:

For the tomato soup:			
4	Tomatoes, diced	2 tsp / 10 ml	Olive oil
2 tbsp / 30 ml	Olive oil	1	Onion, diced
1	Onion, diced	1	Leek, diced
2	Garlic cloves, chopped	50 gm	Spinach
		2	Potatoes, diced
1 tbsp / 15 gm	Tomato paste	4 cups / 1 lt	Water
4 cups / 1 lt	Water	Salt and black pepper to taste	
Salt and black pepper to taste			
For the asparagus soup:		a few	Chervil sprigs
200 gm	Asparagus		

Method:

1. **For the tomato soup,** heat the oil in a pan; sauté the onion, garlic, and tomatoes. Add the tomato paste and water; cook on low heat for 20 minutes. Season to taste. Blend the tomato mixture in a food processor at a very high speed.
2. **For the asparagus soup,** cook the asparagus in water and keep 4 tips aside for garnishing.
3. Heat the oil in a pan; sauté the onion and leek together. Add the asparagus, spinach, potatoes, and water; cook for 20 minutes. Blend the mixture in a food processor at a very high speed.

Service:

Pour the tomato soup in a bowl till half full. Then with the help of a wide spatula, placed at the edge of the bowl, pour the asparagus soup from over the spatula, and then move the spatula towards the middle of the bowl. Garnish with asparagus tips and chervil sprigs.

WINE SUGGESTION: DRY WHITE WINE OR ENTRE DEUX MERS OR CHABLIS

Tomatoes were first cultivated in 700 AD by Aztecs and Incas. Explorers returning from Mexico introduced the tomato into Europe, where it was first mentioned in 1556. The French called it 'the apple of love', the Germans 'the apple of paradise'.

ROASTED TOMATO SOUP WITH GOAT CHEESE QUENELLE

Ingredients:

750 gm	Tomatoes, ripe		crushed
2 tbsp / 30 ml	Olive oil	40 gm	Herbed goat
1 tbsp / 15 gm	Marjoram or thyme		cheese, divided into 2 quenelles
1	Garlic clove,	Salt and black pepper to taste	

Method:

1. Cut the tomatoes into half and squeeze out the seeds.
2. In a baking tray, roast the tomatoes with olive oil at 180°C / 390°F for 30 minutes. Add the marjoram or thyme and garlic. Remove the water that collects in the water tray. Do not discard this water. Roast the tomatoes again for 30 minutes. There should not be any water left in the tray. Season to taste with salt and pepper. Keep 2 roasted tomatoes aside for garnishing.
3. Blend the remaining tomatoes in a food processor and add a little tomato water to give the soup a smooth consistency. Bring the soup to the boil.

Service:

Before seasoning the soup garnish with a roast tomato and a quenelle of goat cheese on each plate.

The phallus-shaped carrot has been associated with stimulation since ancient times and was used by Middle eastern royalty to aid seduction.

MINESTRONE SOUP WITH SEAFOOD

Ingredients:

2	Onions, diced	50 gm	Spaghetti, broken into ½" pieces
I	Leek, diced		
2	Potatoes, diced	2	Zucchini, diced
2	Turnips, diced	2	Garlic cloves, peeled
2	Carrots, diced		
3	Tomatoes, diced	I tbsp / I 5 gm	Basil, chopped
¼ cup / 45 gm	White beans	2	Prawns
½	Cabbage, diced	2	Baby octopus
I 2 cups / 3 lt	Chicken stock or water	4	Mussels
		4	Scallops
Salt to taste		50 gm	Squid rings

Method:

1. In a cooking pot, sauté the onions and leek for 5 minutes. Add the potatoes, turnips, carrots, tomatoes, white beans, and cabbage. Add the chicken stock or water and cook for 20 minutes on low heat. Add salt to taste.
2. Add the spaghetti and zucchini; cook for 5-7 minutes more and then add garlic mixed with basil. Cook for 2 minutes.
3. Bring the mixture to the boil; add the prawns and cook for 5 more minutes. Add the rest of the seafood and cook for 3 more minutes. Serve hot.

Service:

Pour the soup into individual bowls and serve hot.

BLACK BEAN SOUP

Ingredients:

2 cups / 370 gm	Dry black beans		or bone
8 cups / 2 lt	Chicken stock or water	2	Dry red chillies, seeded, chopped
a pinch	Salt	5 tbsp / 20 gm	Fresh coriander, chopped
2	Garlic cloves, chopped	1 tbsp / 20 gm	Soft butter
1	Onion, chopped	40 gm	Bacon, fried till crispy, diced
20 gm	Parsley stalks		
1	Bay leaf	1 tbsp / 20 ml	Cream
90 gm	Ham trimmings		

Method:

1. Soak the beans for 2 hours. Drain and cook in a stockpot with chicken stock, salt, and garlic for 1 hour. Add the onion, parsley stalks, bay leaf, ham trimmings, and dry red chillies; cook for an hour more.
2. If the beans are still not cooked after 2 hours, continue to cook until they turn soft. Season to taste. Remove the ham trimmings and add fresh coriander and butter.

Service:

Pour the soup into individual bowls and garnish with bacon and cream.

COCHIN BLACK TIGER PRAWNS MARINATED TANDOORI WITH EXOTIC FRUIT SALSA

Ingredients:

4	Tiger prawns	½	Apple, peeled, cut into cubes
For the tandoori marinade:			
I cup / 250 gm	Yoghurt	½	Mango, peeled, cut into cubes
2½ tsp / 5 gm	Red chilli powder		
I tsp / 6 gm	Ginger, crushed	I	Tomato, peeled, cut into cubes
I tsp / 6 gm	Garlic, crushed		
½ tsp / 2½ ml	Lemon juice	I	Papaya, small, peeled, cut into cubes
I tsp / 5 ml	Vegetable oil		
1¼ tsp / 2½ gm	Garam masala		
For the fruit salsa:			
½	Kiwi, peeled, cut into small cubes	2½ tbsp / 50 gm	Yoghurt
		2 sprigs	Fresh coriander

Ginger raw, cooked or crystallized is a stimulant to the circulatory system. A stir-fry with freshly grated ginger can stir something spicy in the bedroom later.

Method:

1. **For the tandoori marinade,** mix all the ingredients mentioned. Rub the paste into the prawn and marinate for 4 hours.
2. **For the fruit salsa,** mix all the ingredients together.
3. Cook the prawns in a tandoor or a very hot grill for 5 minutes.

Service:

Arrange a ring of salsa around the plate. Place one prawn in the centre and top with a spoonful of salsa. Repeat the operation a second time. Pour the yoghurt over the salsa ring and garnish with fresh coriander.

(See front cover for picture)

An apple is a tough fruit resistant to diseases. The apple that is supposed to keep the doctor away can be seen as the original aphrodisiac.

MILLE FEUILLE OF GREEN APPLE AND CRAB MEAT WITH GINGER MAYONNAISE

Ingredients:

1½	Green apples, sliced		temperature)
		¼ tsp	Dijon mustard
175 gm	Crab meat	1 tsp / 6 gm	Ginger, chopped
2	Baby carrots	2 tsp / 10 ml	Red wine vinegar
100 gm	Baby onions	½ pinch	Salt
100 gm	Asparagus	1 ½ cups / 375 ml	Vegetable oil
100 gm	Baby corns	**Mix together for vinaigrette dressing:**	
1	Tomato, diced	6 tbsp / 90 ml	Vegetable oil
100 gm	Lettuce leaves	1 tbsp / 15 ml	Red wine vinegar
For the ginger mayonnaise:		a pinch	Salt
½	Egg yolk (room		

Method:

1. **For the ginger mayonnaise,** mix all the ingredients together except the oil. Now pour the oil gently and mix with a whisk until the mixture is thick and shiny. (All the ingredients must be at room temperature for the mayonnaise to rise.)
2. Mix the crab meat with 1 tbsp ginger mayonnaise.
3. Place a slice of green apple on the plate, top with ½ tsp crab meat. Repeat this operation 3 times for each plate (3 slices per plate).
4. Cook all the vegetables in water. Then cool on ice.

Service:

Arrange the lettuce leaves dressed with vinaigrette around the green apple. Put the boiled vegetables around the plate.

GRILLED PRAWN AND GAZPACHO SALSA

Ingredients:

2	Tiger prawns, peeled, deveined	1	Cucumber
		1	Juice of lemon
For the gazpacho salsa:		a pinch each	Paprika, salt, and black pepper
2	Tomatoes		
1	Red capsicum, cut in half, deseeded	1 tbsp / 15 ml	Tabasco sauce
		½ tsp / 2½ ml	Olive oil

Method:

1. Keep ½ tomato, ¼ cucumber, and ¼ capsicum aside for garnishing. Dice the remaining into small cubes.
2. **For the gazpacho salsa,** blend the remaining tomatoes, capsicum, and cucumber in a food processor at high speed. Add lemon juice, paprika, salt, black pepper, Tabasco sauce, and olive oil. A beautiful bright red coloured gazpacho soup will be obtained. Keep the soup in the refrigerator for 1 hour before service.
3. Coat the prawns with salt and paprika. Put a bamboo skewer through the prawn to prevent it from bending. Grill or pan-fry for 3 minutes on each side.

Service:

Pour the gazpacho soup into individual glasses; place the cooked prawn inside tail up and sprinkle diced red capsicum, tomato, and cucumber. Remove the bamboo skewer before serving.

A tropical plant of the nightshade family with fruits containing many seeds. Many coloured varieties of cultivated peppers with edible pungent fruits have been developed.

WINE SUGGESTION: DRY WHITE WINE

Lobster is an exotic food to eat. The rarity of it and the fact that it is very expensive makes it a dish to enjoy on special occasions.

LOBSTER TAIL WITH RED CAPSICUM COULIS AND AVOCADO SALSA

Ingredients:

250 gm	Lobster tail	4 cups / 1 lt	Water
1 each	Onion, carrot, celery stalk, diced	**For the avocado salsa, mix together:**	
For the sauce:		1	Avocado, diced
2 tsp / 10 ml	Olive oil	1	Tomato
1	Red capsicum, diced	½	Onion, chopped
1	Onion, peeled, diced	1	Juice of lemon
		Salt to taste	
		Tabasco sauce to taste	
3	Tomatoes, diced	½ tsp / 3 gm	Ginger, chopped
3	Garlic cloves, peeled		
2 tbsp / 30 gm	Tomato paste	a few	Basil leaves
		1	Slice of toast

Method:

1. Boil the vegetables in 2 lt water for 15 minutes. Dip the lobster tail for 10 minutes. Remove. When cool, peel the shell off.
2. **For the sauce,** heat the oil in a pan; fry the red capsicum, onion, and tomatoes for 5 minutes. Add the garlic and tomato paste. Cook on low heat for 2 minutes and then add water. Cook, uncovered, for 20 minutes more. Add more water, if required. When cooked, remove and blend at high speed for a smooth orange sauce.

Service:

Place the avocado salsa topped with ½ lobster in the centre of each plate. Decorate with fried basil leaves and triangle-shaped toast. Pour the sauce around the avocado.

ATLANTIC SMOKED SALMON AND OYSTER JELLY WITH GINGER AND SOYA DRESSING

Ingredients:

4 slices / 120 gm	Smoked salmons	3 tbsp	Corn
6	Oysters, whole	3 tbsp	Tomatoes, diced
1	Gelatin leaf, finely chopped	2 tbsp / 30 ml	Vinaigrette dressing
100 gm	Mixed lettuce, chopped	1 tsp / 6 gm	Ginger, chopped
		1 tsp / 5 ml	Soya sauce

Method:

1. Make 2 rings of 3½" diameter and ⅓" thick with smoked salmons. Refrigerate.
2. Open the oysters with an oyster knife on top of a glass bowl in order to recuperate the oyster juice coming out of the shells. Strain this white juice (water) through a fine sieve.
3. Melt the gelatin leaf in a small glass of cold water, then in microwave. Add to the oyster juice.
4. Fill the smoked salmon moulds with the juice and refrigerate for 1 hour.
5. Poach the 6 oysters for 30 seconds. Refrigerate.

Service:

Place 2 smoked salmons on each plate over a bed of lettuce. Arrange the oysters around the plate as well as the corn and tomatoes. Dress with vinaigrette mixed with ginger and soya sauce. Chill before serving.

Corns origin is believed to be in the Mexican plateau or in the highlands of Guatemala. It belongs to the grass family. According to Indian legend, corn was of divine origin—'it was the food of the gods that created the earth'.

BUTTERFLY OF SARDINE

Ingredients:

6	Sardine fillets	a few	Mixed lettuce
½	Red capsicum	2-3 tsp	Garlic chives
½	Yellow capsicum	4 tbsp / 60 ml	Vinaigrette
1	Egg, hard-boiled, sliced		dressing

Method:

1. Grill and peel the capsicums. Slice them into thin bands.
2. Grill the sardine under a salamander or on a hot grill for 2 minutes only.

Service:

Arrange the sardine on a plate and decorate with capsicums, egg, mixed lettuce, and garlic chives. Dress with vinaigrette.

Note: *Sardine is a fish with a lot of small bones that can be eaten apart from the main backbone*

Capsicum has been used as a digestive aid to ease intestinal inflammation, stimulate protective mucus membrane of the stomach, and also relieve pain caused by ulcers.

*Caviar, like Aphrodite who was
born from sea foam, comes from
the sea as it is made of fish egg. It
is an aphrodisiac and is eaten on
special occasions.*

GRILLED SCALLOPS WITH WASABI VINAIGRETTE AND CAVIAR BUTTER SAUCE

Ingredients:

10	Scallops (no roe)		cooked
For the wasabi vinaigrette:			
2 gm	Wasabi powder	50 gm	Spring onions
3 tbsp / 45 ml	Vegetable oil	2½ tbsp / 50 ml	Cream
½ tsp	Dijon mustard	2½ tbsp / 50 gm	Butter
1 tbsp / 15 ml	Red wine vinegar	½	Juice of lemon
Salt and black pepper to taste		25 gm	Caviar Suruga
25 gm	Small caper,	15 gm	Chervil sprigs

Method:

1. **For the wasabi vinaigrette,** mix the first 5 ingredients together. Add the caper and keep aside.
2. Cook the spring onions in boiling water. Remove and keep warm.
3. Boil the cream in a small saucepan; add the butter and mix gently with a whisk. Remove from heat and add lemon juice.
4. Cook the scallops on a very hot grill for about 1 minute on each side.

Service:

Place 5 scallops on each plate. Sprinkle with wasabi vinaigrette. Place the caviar on top of the scallops. Pour the butter sauce over it. Place 2 spring onions on each plate and serve garnished with chervil sprigs.

This erotic, sensual fruit has a moist flesh. There are hundreds of varieties of mangoes which are extremely popular in India, Mexico, and the Caribbean.

LAMB CHOP TANDOORI AND MANGO CHUTNEY

Ingredients:

2	Lamb chops, trimmed	3-4 tbsp / 45-60 ml	Vegetable oil
For the tandoori marinade:		**For the mango chutney:**	
4 tbsp / 80 gm	Yoghurt	1	Mango, peeled, diced
½ tsp / 1 gm	Red chilli powder	½	Onion, chopped
1 tbsp / 18 gm	Ginger-garlic paste	1 tsp / 6 gm	Ginger, chopped
		1 tsp / 5 gm	Brown sugar
2½ tsp / 5 gm	Garam masala	4 tsp / 20 ml	Vinegar
a pinch	Salt	**For the herbed cream:**	
1	Juice of lemon	3 tbsp / 60 ml	Cream, whipped
a few drops	Red or yellow colour	½ tsp / 3 gm	Garlic, chopped
		2 tsp	Herbs, chopped

Method:

1. **For the tandoori marinade,** mix all the ingredients together and rub into the lamb chops. Marinate for 3-4 hours.
2. **For the mango chutney,** sauté the onion and ginger for 2-3 minutes in a little oil on low heat. Add the sugar and vinegar. Cook for 3 more minutes. Add the mango and cook for 2 more minutes. Keep warm.
3. **For the herbed cream,** mix the cream, garlic, and herbs together.
4. Remove the lamb chops from the marinade. Cook the lamb chops in a tandoor or frying pan for 5-6 minutes on medium heat.

Service:

Place the chutney in a glass, pour the herbed cream over the chutney and keep the lamb chop on top.

WINE SUGGESTION:
BEAUJOLAIS OR CÔTES
DU RHONE

The Aztecs called the avocado tree Ahuacuatl which means testicle tree. The ancients thought the fruit hanging in pairs on the trees resembled the testicles.

HERBED GOAT CHEESE IN PHYLLO PASTRY

Ingredients:

½ cup / 60 gm	Goat cheese, fresh	1 tbsp / 12 gm	Garlic, chopped
		Tabasco sauce to taste	
6 sheets	Pyhllo pastry, 5 x 7" (available in the market)	2 tbsp	Tomato, diced
		2 tbsp	Avocado, diced
		Lemon juice to taste	
1 tbsp	Herbs, chopped	Salt and black pepper to taste	

Method:

1. Mix the goat cheese, herbs, garlic, and Tabasco together in a stainless-steel bowl.
2. Place the phyllo sheet on the table. Pipe the goat cheese mixture in the centre of the pastry and roll like a cigarette. Repeat with the other sheets. Cook for 5 minutes in a hot oven at 220°C / 470°F.
3. Mix the tomato, avocado, lemon juice, and salt and pepper together.

Service

Divide the vegetable mixture into two portions. Put a portion in each glass with three cigarettes of cheese inside. Repeat with the other glass.

WINE SUGGESTION:
DRY WHITE WINE

PORK DIM SUMS IN CABBAGE LEAVES

Ingredients:

2	Cabbage leaves	**For the salsa:**	
For the filling:		4 tbsp	Pineapple, diced
150 gm	Pork mince	4 tbsp	Tomato, diced
1 tbsp / 12 gm	Garlic, chopped	2 tbsp	Garlic chives,
a pinch each	Clove, mace, and		chopped
	coriander powder		
½ tsp / 2½ ml	Cognac	1 ½ tbsp / 22 ml	Light soya sauce
Salt and black pepper to taste			

Method:

1. Boil the cabbage leaves for 30 seconds in water. Remove and then cool in ice water to retain the bright green colour of the cabbage. Drain on a dry cloth.
2. **For the filling,** mix the pork mince, garlic, clove, mace, coriander powder, and cognac together. Add salt and black pepper to taste.
3. Place 1 tbsp filling in the centre of each cabbage leaf, and fold the leaf like an envelope. Secure with a string of garlic chive. Cook the dim sums in steam or boiling water for 10 minutes.
4. **For the salsa,** mix the pineapple, tomato, and garlic chives together. Season to taste.

Service:

Place half the salsa in a glass, with a dim sum over it. Serve with soya sauce on the side.

main course

According to traditional Indian herbal medicine, a nightcap of powdered cardamom that has been boiled with milk and mixed with honey can help cure impotence and premature ejaculation.

KOCHI PRAWN AND COCONUT CURRY

Ingredients:

300 gm	Prawns	4	Green chillies, chopped
1 cup / 250 ml	Coconut milk		
3 tbsp / 45 ml	Mustard oil	**Crush to a paste:**	
1	Bay leaf	½"	Ginger
1	Cinnamon stick, 1" piece	6	Garlic cloves
		½ tsp / 1 gm	Cumin seeds
2	Cloves		
4	Green cardamoms, bruised	a few threads	Saffron
		2	Tomatoes, diced
		2 sprigs	Fresh coriander
1	Onion, chopped		

Method:

1. Heat the oil in a pan; sauté the bay leaf, cinnamon stick, cloves, and green cardamoms for about 2 minutes. Add the onion and sauté on low heat for 4 minutes.
2. Add the green chillies and ginger-garlic-cumin paste. Sauté for 3 minutes; add the saffron and 1 cup water. Season to taste.
3. Add the prawns and simmer for 10 minutes. Add the coconut milk and cook on low heat for 2 more minutes, but do not boil the curry to prevent it from curdling.

Service:

Garnish the prawns with tomatoes and coriander sprigs.

LOBSTER TANDOORI WITH DRY FRUIT BIRYANI AND PICKLED BABY OCTOPUS

Ingredients:

2	Lobsters, peeled

For the tandoori marinade:

4 tbsp / 80 gm	Yoghurt
½ tsp / 1 gm	Red chilli powder
1 tbsp / 18 gm	Ginger-garlic paste
1 tsp / 2 gm	Garam masala
Salt to taste	
1	Juice of lemon
3 tbsp / 45 ml	Vegetable oil

For the pickled baby octopus:

²/₃ cup / 150 ml	Vegetable oil
5 tsp / 15 gm	Black mustard seeds
4	Star anise
5 tsp / 10 gm	Cumin seeds
7 tsp / 15 gm	Dry fennel
5	Dry red chillies, whole
¾ tsp	Curry leaves
¼ cup / 30 gm	Onions, chopped
2 tbsp / 36 gm	Ginger-garlic paste
5 tsp / 10 gm	Red chilli powder
2½ tsp / 5 gm	Turmeric powder
Salt to taste	
200 gm	Baby octopus, whole
7 tbsp / 105 ml	White vinegar
¼ cup / 60 gm	Sugar

For the biryani:

1 cup / 155 gm	Basmati rice
½ cup / 175 ml	Vegetable oil
2 tbsp / 24 gm	Ghee
2	Cloves
1	Bay leaf
1	Cinnamon stick, 1" piece
3	Green cardamoms
1	Onion, sliced
2	Green chillies, sliced
250 gm	Ginger-garlic paste
4 cups / 1 lt	Chicken stock or water
Lemon juice to taste	
Salt to taste	
a few sprigs	Fresh coriander
a few	Mint leaves
¼ cup / 30 gm	Raisins
¼ cup / 30 gm	Pistachios
¼ cup / 30 gm	Dry apricots
a few drops	Yellow colour

Fennel seeds are a common ingredient for flavouring stocks and sauces. Used as an effective digestive, they freshen and sweeten the breath.

WINE SUGGESTION: ROSÉ WINE, DRY WHITE WINE OR BEAUJOLAIS STYLE WINE

Method:

1. **For the tandoori marinade,** mix all the ingredients and rub into the lobsters. Marinate for 3-4 hours. Keep refrigerated.
2. Cook the lobsters in a tandoor or very hot oven for 10 minutes.
3. **For the pickled baby octopus,** heat the oil in a saucepan to smoking point. Crackle together mustard seeds, star anise, cumin seeds, dry fennel, dry red chillies, and curry leaves. Keep aside. Add the onions and sauté till golden brown.
4. Add the ginger-garlic paste and simmer again for a few minutes. Add the red chilli powder, turmeric powder, and salt to taste.
5. Add the octopus and sauté. Add white vinegar and sugar and cook on low heat for 10 minutes. Reduce the mixture to $^1/_3$.
6. **For the biryani,** heat the oil and ghee together. Add the cloves, bay leaf, cinnamon sticks, and green cardamom; sauté until they crackle. Add the onion and green chillies; cook until brown. Add ginger-garlic paste and cook for 5 minutes.
7. Add the chicken stock or water and rice; cook for 5 minutes. (The amount of liquid must be of 1 $^2/_3$ the amount of rice.)
8. Add lemon juice, salt, fresh coriander, mint leaves, and dry fruits. Add colour, remove from heat and cover the dish with a lid; let it rest for 1 hour.

Service:

Cut each lobster into half and keep on the plate with the biryani on one side and pickled octopus on the other.

Raita (yoghurt mixed with diced tomato, cucumber, and chopped mint) can be served separately.

PEPPERCORN STEAKS WITH ANCHOVIES AND FRESH HERBS

Ingredients:

2 (220 gm each)	Beef steaks	4 tbsp / 80 gm	Butter
8	Anchovies, fillets in can, drained	1	Juice of lemon
		½ tsp	Thyme
1 cup / 250 ml	Milk	½ tsp	Parsley, chopped
Salt to taste		½ tsp	Sage, chopped
2 tsp / 12 gm	Black peppercorns, cracked	½ tsp / 1 ½ gm	Garlic, chopped
		1 tbsp / 15 ml	Worcestershire sauce

Method:

1. Soak the anchovy fillets in milk for 20 minutes. Drain and pat dry with paper towel.
2. Season the steaks with salt and black pepper.
3. Melt 2 tbsp butter in a pan on medium heat. When the butter starts to turn brown, add the steaks and cook for 3 minutes on each side. Remove the steak from the pan and keep warm. Drain the butter from the pan. Add the anchovy fillets and let them dissolve on medium heat. Add the remaining butter, lemon juice, herbs, garlic, and Worcestershire sauce; mix well.

Service:

Place a steak on the plate and pour the sauce over it. Serve with roasted potatoes and mixed lettuce.

According to the 'The Perfumed Garden' (an ancient Arabic love manual), ground pepper mixed with cardamom or lavender, galangal, musk and honey is a potent topical aphrodisiac for men. In India, peppercorns are crushed with almonds, mixed with milk and consumed as an aphrodisiac.

The heat in garlic is said to stir sexual desires. Garlic has been used for centuries to cure everything from a common cold to heart ailments.

SEAFOOD FETTUCCINE WITH BLACK INK SAUCE

Ingredients:

240 gm	Fettuccini, fresh or dry	2	Baby octopus, cleaned
2 cups / 500 ml	Red wine sauce*	60 gm	Squid rings, cut
60 gm	Black squid ink	4	Scallops, cleaned
1 tbsp / 20 gm	Butter	4	Mussels
1 tbsp / 15 ml	Olive oil	½ tsp / 3 gm	Garlic, chopped
4 small / 2 large	Prawns, cut into half	½ bunch	Basil leaves
		6	Cherry tomatoes

Method:

1. Boil the red wine sauce and black squid ink together. Keep warm.
2. Boil the fettuccini with salt and a little oil. While cooking, keep stirring the pasta to prevent them from sticking together.
3. Meanwhile, heat the butter and olive oil in a frying pan; sauté the seafood together starting with the prawns, then 2 minutes later add baby octopus, squid rings, and finally, scallops. Add the garlic and cook for 1 more minute.

Service:

Place the fettuccine in the centre of the plate, add seafood on top, and pour the wine sauce around. Garnish with basil and tomatoes.

Note: *For the red wine sauce: roast 1 carrot, chopped; ½ onion, chopped; ½ garlic head, chopped and 1 bay leaf in the oven for 10 minutes. Add ⅓ lt of red wine. Reduce till dry. Add ⅓ lt of chicken stock or water. Cook for 15 minutes or till reduced to syrupy consistency.*

CORN FED CHICKEN POT AU FEU WITH SPINACH

Ingredients:

2	Half corn fed chicken with skin	1	Carrot, peeled
		1	Turnip, peeled
4 cups / 1 lt	Chicken stock	1	Beetroot, peeled
1	Onion	200 gm	Spinach
Salt to taste		Fresh chervil leaves	

Method:

1. Cut the half chicken into 4 pieces (2 pieces in the leg, 2 pieces in the breast). Bring the chicken stock to the boil and cook the chicken in it for 20 minutes with the onion. Add salt to taste.
2. Add the vegetables, cut into small barrel shape. Cook for 10 minutes and remove the chicken and vegetables out of the stock.
3. Keep the stock boiling on the stove. Boil the spinach leaves in the stock and blend with a hand blender. Keep warm.

Service:

Place the vegetable and chicken pieces on the plate. Pour the green sauce around it. Garnish with fresh chervil leaves.

WINE SUGGESTION: WHITE WINE OR BEAUJOLAIS STYLE

Cinnamon sticks are made from long pieces of bark. They are rolled, pressed and dried. Cinnamon has a sweet, woody fragrance in both ground and stick forms.

ROAST BREAST OF DUCK WITH RED WINE AND SPICES

Ingredients:

1 (1.6 kg)	Duck		market)
10 gm	Cloves	**For the wine sauce:**	
10 gm	Mace	1	Carrot, diced
10 gm	Cinnamon sticks	1	Onion, diced
1 tsp / 6 gm	White peppercorns	1	Bay leaf
		2½ tbsp / 30 gm	Garlic, unpeeled
Salt to taste		2 cups / 500 ml	Water or stock
2 cups / 500 ml	Red wine		
2	Onions, finely chopped	2 tbsp / 40 gm	Butter
		300 gm	Pak choy
1 head	Garlic	100 gm	Mixed lettuce
150 gm	Puff pastry (available in the	1 tbsp / 15 ml	Vinegar
		3 tbsp / 45 ml	Vegetable oil

Method:

1. Coarsely powder the cloves, mace, cinnamon sticks, white peppercorns, and salt together.
2. Coat the duck with the spice mixture and roast in the oven for 25 minutes at 190°C / 410°F. Remove from the oven and debone. Keep the breasts warm.
3. Debone the legs of the duck and chop the meat finely. Cook the meat in the red wine for 20 minutes. The red wine should be reduced to an almost dry consistency.
3. Add the onions and garlic; cook for 10 more minutes on low heat. The mixture will look like a thick purée.
4. Roll out the puff pastry and cut 4 discs 1¼" wide. Put 1 tbsp of duck mince in the centre of one disc; seal the filling inside by placing another disc on top. Repeat with the second disc. Cook

WINE SUGGESTION: RED BORDEAU OR
A BURGUNDY OR NEW WORLD WINE LIKE CABERNET OR SHIRAZ

for 12 minutes in the oven at 180°C / 390°F. When cooked, keep warm.

5. **For the sauce,** cut the duck bones into small pieces and roast in the oven for 15 minutes. Add the carrot, onion, bay leaf, the rest of the spices and more garlic. Roast in the oven for 10 more minutes. Remove from oven. Add the rest of the wine and boil until the wine is completely evaporated. Add the water or chicken stock and cook the sauce for 20 minutes more on low heat to prevent the liquid from evaporating completely. Pass through a sieve and keep warm.

6. Melt the butter in a pan; fry the pak choy for a few seconds. Season to taste. Warm the duck breasts for 5 minutes before serving.

Service:

Place the sautéed pak choy on the side of a plate, and the sliced duck breasts on the base of the pak choy. Pour the sauce over the duck breasts and place the pie of duck legs on the head of the plate. Arrange a bunch of mixed lettuce on the side of the puff pastry already dressed with vinaigrette.

PEKING DUCK RISOTTO

Ingredients:

200 gm	Peking duck (keep the skin aside for garnishing), cooked	I tbsp / 20 gm	Butter
		¾ cup / 125 gm	Risotto rice
		75 gm	Asparagus tips
		I tbsp / 30 gm	Parmesan cheese
		I ½ tbsp / 40 gm	Spring onions, chopped
I cup / 250 ml	Duck stock		
½ cup / 60 gm	Onions, chopped		

Method:

1. Separate the duck meat from the bones. Cut the meat into small strips 1½" long.
2. Cut the duck bones into small pieces, and place them in a cooking pot. Add cold water and bring to the boil, cook for 35 minutes. Strain and keep the Peking duck stock hot.
3. In a saucepan that can fit in the oven, fry the onions with I tsp butter. Add the risotto rice. Cook on low heat until the onions turn translucent (3-4 minutes).
4. Add the Peking duck stock, asparagus tips, and duck meat. Cover and cook in the oven for 18 minutes at 180°C / 390°F.
5. After 18 minutes, mix the rice with a fork and add Parmesan cheese and the remaining butter. Serve onto each plate.

Service:

Sprinkle with 15 gm spring onion and Peking duck skin cut into strips.

(See p. 42 for picture)

Given its phallic shape, asparagus is frequently enjoyed as an aphrodisiac food.

A squash having an elongated shape and a smooth, thin, dark green rind. One cup of zucchini has about 35 calories. It contains about 340 milligrams of potassium and 70 milligrams of phosphorus.

ROAST GUINEA FOWL WITH SALMON FILLET CONFIT AND RED WINE

Ingredients:

1 (1.2 kg)	Guinea fowl	4 cups / 1 lt	Water or chicken stock (optional)
2 (100 gm each)	Salmon fillets		
1	Bones of Salmon	**For the zucchini timbale:**	
2 cups / 500 ml	Red wine	1	Zucchini, sliced into 2 thin band layers
2	Tomatoes, chopped		
60 gm	Mushrooms, chopped, cooked	2 cups / 500 ml	Olive oil
For the sauce:		80 gm	Mixed lettuce
1	Onion, diced	2 tbsp / 30 ml	Vinaigrette dressing
1	Carrot, diced		
1 head	Garlic, unpeeled		

Method:

1. Roast the guinea fowl in the oven for 15 minutes at 200°C / 430°F. Remove the legs and breasts from the bones. Keep the breasts warm.
2. Dice the leg meat and cook in 1 cup red wine for 20 minutes. Strain the wine and keep the meat warm. Mix the meat with 2 tbsp tomatoes and mushrooms. Cook the mixture for 5 more minutes on low heat.
3. **For the sauce**, dice all the guinea fowl bones and salmon bones. Roast together for 10 minutes in the oven. Then add the onion, carrot, and garlic. Roast again for 5 more minutes.
4. Remove from the oven and add the remaining wine. Boil until the wine evaporates. Add the water or chicken stock. Cook for 20 minutes on low heat. Pass the mixture through a fine sieve. Keep aside.

WINE SUGGESTION: BURGUNDY OR BEAUJOLAIS

4. **For the zucchini timbale,** pan-fry the zucchini for 30 seconds on each side. Place the zucchini in a stainless-steel ring, then add the diced leg meat in the centre of the ring and the remaining tomatoes on top. Keep in a warm oven for 2 minutes.
5. Heat the olive oil to 80°C / 130°F in a small pot; carefully lower the salmon fillets. The salmon fillets have to be completely submerged in oil. Cook for 8 minutes. The salmon will not be fat but very moist if you keep the oil temperature at 80°C.

Service:

Place the guinea fowl breast, the salmon fillets, zucchini timbale, and baby lettuce dressed with vinaigrette on a plate. Pour the sauce over the guinea fowl.

ROAST RACK OF LAMB WITH ONION MASALA AND EGGPLANT

Ingredients:

1	Rack of lamb of eight bones each		1" piece
		1	Whole star anise
For the marinade:		½	Bay leaf
½ tsp / 3 gm	Garlic, crushed	1 tbsp / 15 gm	Tomato paste
½ tsp / 3 gm	Ginger, crushed	Salt to taste	
½ tsp / 3 gm	Chilli paste	**For the eggplant cake:**	
½ tbsp / 7½ ml	Vegetable oil	250 gm	Eggplants, cut into half
For the onion masala :		1½ tbsp / 22 ml	Olive oil
2	Onions, sliced	Salt and black pepper to taste	
½ tsp / 3 gm	Garlic, crushed	2 tbsp / 24 gm	Garlic, chopped
½ tsp / 3 gm	Ginger, crushed	25 gm	Tarragon
½ tsp / 3 gm	Chilli paste	1	Egg
1 tsp / 1½ gm	Coriander powder	1¾ tbsp / 26 gm	Breadcrumbs
½ tsp / 1½ gm	Cumin powder	2 tsp / 10 ml	Cream
¾ tsp	Turmeric powder	**For the sauce:**	
Whole spices:		½	Carrot, diced
1½	Cloves	½	Celery stems, diced
2	Green coriander pods	½	Garlic bulb, peeled
1½	Black cardamom pods	1 cup / 250 ml	Water or lamb stock
1	Cinnamon stick,		

Method:

1. **For the marinade,** combine all the ingredients and rub into the lamb racks. Keep aside for 3 hours.

2. **For the onion masala,** combine all the spice ingredients and grind to a smooth paste.

3. Heat 1 tbsp oil in a casserole dish or a heavy-based pan just large enough to hold the lamb racks. Sauté the whole spices for 2-3 minutes, then add the onion masala and sauté until the oil separates. Add the tomato paste and salt; mix well. Add the lamb.

4. Remove from heat and cook for 12 minutes in a medium-hot oven at 180°C / 390°F.

5. **For the eggplant cake,** sprinkle some salt, black pepper, and olive oil over the eggplants. Cook in the oven for 10 minutes in a baking tray.

6. Then pull the eggplant flesh out of the skin and blend the flesh in a food processor with the remaining ingredients. Pour the mixture into 4 round ceramic or aluminium moulds 3" wide and 1"' high. Cook in a bain-marie (a vessel of hot water in which a dish of food is placed for slow cooking) for 20 minutes. Keep aside.

7. Take the lamb racks out of the oven. Keep them aside.

8. **For the sauce,** cook all the ingredients for 15 minutes on low heat. Strain the liquid and season with salt.

Service:

Place an eggplant cake in the centre of each plate with one rack of lamb on top. Arrange the onion masala around and pour the sauce over the meat.

LAMB LOIN FILLED WITH MUSHROOMS AND WRAPPED IN PUFF PASTRY

Originating in ancient Rome, mushroom has long been valued for its medicinal properties (it was thought to be a blood purifier). There are so many varieties of mushrooms, both edible and toxic, that mass consumption is limited to those commercially-grown varieties which can be trusted to be edible.

Ingredients:

I	Lamb loin, debonned. Keep bones for sauce	I 2	Onion, diced Garlic cloves, chopped
I tbsp / 20 gm	Butter	2 cups / 500 ml	Chicken stock or water
½	Onion, chopped		
150 gm	Mushrooms, finely chopped	100 gm	Mushrooms
300 gm	Puff pastry	I	Artichoke, peeled
For the sauce:		4	Baby carrots
I	Carrot, diced	2	Potatoes

Method:

1. Seal (fry in hot oil to brown) lamb loin for 1 minute on each side.
2. Heat the butter in a pan; add the onion and sauté for 2 minutes. Then add the mushrooms and cook for 10 minutes.
3. Cut the lamb loin in half (lengthwise) and fill the bottom half with the cooked mushrooms. Cover with the top half and wrap in puff pastry. Decorate the puff pastry on top, then egg wash and cook in the oven at 200°C / 430°F for 8 minutes.
4. **For the sauce,** in a roasting tray, bake the carrot, onion, garlic, and lamb bones for 30 minutes. Remove from oven and add the chicken stock or water and boil for 20 minutes; strain.
5. Boil all the vegetables and then sauté in 1 tbsp butter.

Service:

Cut lamb loin in 2 halves. Place a ½ on each plate and surround with vegetables. Pour sauce over the vegetables and garnish with celery.

Black olives are the ripe, small fruits of trees that are native to Mediterranean Europe. Ripe olives are cured in salt, seasonings, brines, vinegars, and oils and have a pungent flavour.

TENDERLOIN OF BEEF WITH BLACK OLIVE SAUCE AND ROAST VEGETABLES

Ingredients:

2 (160 gm each)	Tenderloin of beef	2	Potatoes, peeled, shaped into small barrels
For the red wine sauce:			
300 gm	Beef or chicken bones, cut into small pieces	60 gm	Pork mince
		1	Egg yolk
		1 tsp / 3 gm	Garlic, chopped
1	Carrot, diced	1 tsp / 5 ml	Brandy
1	Onion, cut into large pieces	1 tbsp / 15 gm	Breadcrumbs
		2 cups / 500 ml	Olive oil
1 cup / 250 ml	Red wine	2	Tomatoes
2 cups / 500 ml	Water or chicken stocks	2	Leeks, cut into 1"- long slices
50 gm	Black olives, depitted, finely chopped	1 tbsp / 20 gm	Butter
		a few leaves	Baby lettuce
		1 sprig	Rosemary

Method:

1. **For the red wine sauce,** roast the beef or chicken bones in the oven for 20 minutes at 200°C / 430°F. Then add the carrot and onion. Cook for 15 minutes more.
2. Remove from the oven and place on open fire. Discard the excess fat and add the red wine. Bring the mixture to the boil. Cook until the mixture is dry. Avoid burning the pan. When the red wine is completely reduced, add the water or chicken stock and cook for 15 minutes more.
3. The sauce should be brown and reduced to about 1 cup. Add some water, if you don't have the required quantity. Pass the liquid through a fine sieve. Add the black olives and keep warm.

4. Carve a cavity in the centre of the potato barrels.
5. Mix the pork mince with egg yolk, garlic, and brandy. Stuff this mixture into the cavity. Add breadcrumbs on top.
6. Bake the potatoes in olive oil in the oven for 20 minutes. Add the tomatoes and cook together for 5 more minutes.
7. Cook the leeks in boiling water. Remove and toss them in butter.

Service:

Grill or pan-fry the tenderloin of beef for 10 minutes on medium heat. Place on a plate with stuffed potato, roast tomato, and leeks. Pour the red wine sauce over the meat and garnish with baby lettuce and rosemary.

IMAM BAYALDI

Ingredients:

2	Eggplants, cut into half	2	Tomatoes, ripe
		½	Juice of lemon
½ cup / 175 ml	Olive oil	60 gm	Herbs, chopped, mixed with 2 tbsp breadcrumbs
Salt to taste			
1	Onion, chopped		
1	Bay leaf	2 tbsp / 40 gm	Butter, melted
1	Garlic clove, chopped	Parmesan cheese to taste	
		a few	Mixed lettuce
50 gm	Mushrooms, chopped	1 tbsp / 15 ml	Vinaigrette dressing

Bay leaf, an aromatic dried leaf of the bay tree, is an evergreen Mediterranean shrub with deep green leaves and purple berries.

Method:

1. Sprinkle some olive oil and salt on the eggplants and cook in the oven for 20 minutes. Remove from the oven and scoop out the eggplant flesh. Keep the half shells aside.
2. In a sauté pan, fry the onion, bay leaf, garlic, and mushrooms for 3 minutes. Add the tomatoes and eggplant flesh and cook for 5 more minutes. Add lemon juice.
3. Place the eggplant shells into a baking tray, filled with eggplant mixture and sprinkle some olive oil. Top with breadcrumbs and herbs. Pour in the butter and bake in the oven at 160°C / 350°F for 1 hour 15 minutes.

Service:

When cooked, sprinkle some Parmesan cheese and garnish with mixed lettuce dressed with vinaigrette.

BABY ONION TARTS WITH CABERNET SAUCE AND BALSAMIC REDUCTION

Ingredients:

200 gm	Baby shallots or baby onions, peeled	I	Egg
		a pinch	Salt
		For the Cabernet sauce:	
2 cups / 500 ml	Red wine	I cup / 250 ml	Balsamic vinegar
I	Bay leaf	½ cup / 60 gm	Fresh herbed goat cheese
Salt and black pepper to taste			
For the 200 gm shortcrust pastry:		60 gm	Baby lettuce
I cup / 125 gm	Refined flour	3 tbsp / 45 ml	Vinaigrette dressing
I cup / 200 gm	Soft butter		

Method:

1. Cook the baby onions in a pan with I cup red wine, bay leaf, salt, and black pepper for 20 minutes. Drain the wine completely when the onions turn soft.
2. **For the 200 gm shortcrust pastry,** mix the 2 ingredients together. Knead the dough gently for 2 minutes and refrigerate for 2 hours.
3. Roll out the shortcrust pastry dough and cut 2 discs, each 4" wide and 2 mm thick. Place them in non-stick 3½" moulds.
4. Place half the baby onion mixture in each mould and cook in the oven for 15-20 minutes at 180°C / 390°F.
5. **For the Cabernet sauce,** mix the remaining red wine and balsamic vinegar together. Boil on low heat until syrupy.

Service:

Remove the tarts from the moulds and place individually in the centre of each plate. Top with half of the goat cheese and a few baby lettuce dressed with vinaigrette. Pour half the sauce around the tart.

Onion, a common ingredient in almost all cuisines, has been used for thousands of years as an aphrodisiac. It is recommended in both ancient Hindu and Arabic texts on the art of making love.

ROAST PEAR AND BLUE CHEESE TART

Ingredients:

2	Pears		wash)
125 gm	Puff pastry (available in the market)	100 gm	Blue cheese, Bresse blue or Danish blue
1	Egg, whisked (egg		

Method:

1. Roll the puff pastry out into 2 mm thickness. Cut into 4 discs with a round cutter 5" diameter. Prick each disc with a fork several times.
2. Peel and slice the pears. Arrange the slices neatly on each disc ½ cm from the edge.
3. Brush the pears with the egg (egg wash).

Service:

Cover the pear with blue cheese and bake for 12 minutes at 180°C / 390°F.

Pear is s sweet juicy yellow or green fruit with a rounded shape that becomes narrower towards the stalk. Pears are good for the skin and contain plenty of fibers.

PAK CHOY GINGER AND RICOTTA GNOCCHI

Ginger is a knobby rhizome, known for its sharp, pungent, cleansing taste and its digestive properties. Its tan potato-like skin is usually peeled away after which it is grated, sliced or chopped.

Ingredients:

1 ½ cups / 180 gm	Ricotta cheese	2	Eggs
100 gm	Pak choy	Salt and black pepper to taste	
2 tbsp / 20 gm	Refined flour	2 tsp / 10 ml	Olive oil
1 tsp / 6 gm	Ginger, chopped	6 tbsp / 120 gm	Butter
3 tbsp / 90 gm	Parmesan cheese, grated	a few	Basil leaves.

Method:

1. Drain the ricotta through a fine sieve.
2. Mix the pak choy, refined flour, ginger, parmesan cheese, eggs, salt and black pepper with the riccota.
3. On a flat surface, shape the ricotta mixture into small balls and cook them in boiling water for 5 minutes. The gnocchi are cooked when they rise to the surface of the water. Remove when cooked and drain on a cloth.
4. Pan fry the gnocchi with olive oil and butter for a minute or two.

Service:

Transfer the gnocchi onto 2 plates and garnish with parmesan cheese, basil leaves, and a dash of live oil. Eat very hot.

SPAGHETTINI WITH TOMATO AND SAFFRON 'PESTO'

Ingredients:

250 gm	Tomatoes, ripe	½ cup / 175 ml	Olive oil
250 gm	Spaghetti	Salt and black pepper to taste	
a pinch	Saffron, ground	a few	Parsley, chopped
1 cup / 125 gm	Pecorino cheese, aged, grated	a few	Basil leaves, chopped

Method:

1. Remove the skin from the tomatoes and cut them into large pieces. Remove the seeds. Place the tomatoes in a stainless-steel bowl and mash them with a fork. Add the saffron, half the cheese, olive oil, and salt and pepper to taste. Mix well with a wooden spoon. Refrigerate for 1 hour before service.
2. Bring a pot of water to the boil; add salt and a dash of olive oil. Cook the spaghetti for about 4 minutes or until done to your liking. Drain.

Service:

Transfer the spaghetti onto 2 plates. Pour the cooled tomato sauce over the spaghetti, sprinkle the remaining cheese, parsley, basil, and a dash of olive oil.

Cheese has a long history and was prized by the ancient Egyptians, Greeks and Romans who believe that it could cure many ills, ranging from impotence to constipation.

WINE SUGGESTION: DRY WHITE WINE

desserts

Almond is a symbol of fertility. The aroma is thought to induce passion in women.

DARK ALMOND CHOCOLATE TART

Ingredients:

For the shortcrust almond pastry:		5 tbsp / 100 gm	Butter, unsalted
2½ tbsp / 50 gm	Butter	**For the glaze *noir*:**	
10 tbsp / 200 gm	Icing sugar	2 tsp / 10 ml	Water
1	Egg	1 tsp / 5 ml	Cream
¾ cup / 90 gm	Refined flour	1 tsp / 5 gm	Caster sugar
5 tbsp / 75 gm	Almond powder	2 gm	Liquid glucose
For the chocolate tart filling:		2 gm	Cocoa powder
1⅛ cups / 125 ml	Cream	2½ gm	Gelatin leaves, soaked in hot water
270 gm	Cooking chocolate		

Method:

1. **For the shortcrust almond pastry,** whip the butter and sugar till fluffy. Add the egg, flour, and almond powder. Fold together gently.
2. **For the chocolate tart filling,** simmer the cream, remove from heat and add chocolate and butter. Mix well. Strain and keep aside.
3. **For the glaze *noir*,** boil the water, cream, caster sugar, and glucose together. Add the cocoa powder and boil till 140°C / 310°F. Add the gelatin mixture. Strain.
4. Roll out the almond pastry on a floured surface to 3 mm thickness. Line the tart mould 1¼ × 2½ diameter with the pastry. Bake at 180°C / 390°F till fully done.
5. Fill in the prepared chocolate filling and refrigerate for 3-4 hours.

Service:

Before serving pour some cocoa glaze over the tarts.

'MENDIANTS' POORMAN'S CHOCOLATE TRUFFLE

The Aztecs referred to chocolate as 'the nourishment of the gods.' Chocolates contain chemicals thought to effect neurotransmitter in the brain and a related substance to caffeine called theobromine.

Ingredients:

150 gm	*Dark chocolate*	*½ cup / 60 gm*	*Walnuts, chopped*
½ cup / 60 gm	*Almonds, sliced*		
½ cup / 60 gm	*Pistachios, shelled, peeled*	*½ cup / 60 gm*	*Raisins, soaked in rum (or water)*

Method:

1. Put the chocolate in a small heat-resistant glass bowl and place in a pan half filled with water.
2. Slowly bring the water to the boil to melt the chocolate. Keep the water simmering until the chocolate melts.
3. Roast the nuts in the oven at 200°C / 430°F for 10 minutes. Remove and mix with soaked raisins. With a teaspoon place a few dollops of chocolate on a greaseproof paper, on a baking tray, and then sprinkle the nut and raisin mixture over the dollops before the chocolate cools. Serve cold.

All kinds of eggs from chicken to fish eggs (caviar) have been thought of as fertility symbols and by extension aphrodisiacs.

WARM CHOCOLATE FONDANT AND FRESH STRAWBERRIES

Ingredients:

80 gm + 30 gm	Cooking chocolate, slab	¾ cup / 90 gm	Refined flour
3	Eggs	300 gm	Strawberries, whole
¾ cup / 150 gm	Sugar	2 scoops	Chocolate ice cream
5 tbsp / 100 gm	Butter, melted		

Method:

1. Beat the eggs and sugar together in a bowl until the mixture is creamy. Add 80 gm melted chocolate and all the butter. Lastly, add the flour. Mix well.
2. Pour the mixture into 2 non-stick moulds 2½" in diameter. Bake in the oven for 8 minutes at 200°C / 430°F.

Service:

Place the hot cakes on individual plates and pour 30 gm melted chocolate over them. Place the strawberries around the cakes and a scoop of chocolate ice cream on top of each cake.

FRESH STRAWBERRY TART WITH CRÈME BRULÈE MOUSSE

Ingredients:

Butter is a pale yellow edible fatty substance made by churning cream and is used as a spread or in cooking.

For the sablé pastry:

2 tbsp / 40 gm	Sugar
2	Egg yolks
1 tbsp / 15 gm	Baking powder
a pinch	Salt
4 tbsp / 40 gm	Refined flour
3 tbsp / 60 gm	Butter

For the crème brulée:

2 cups / 500 ml	Milk (full cream)
2½ tbsp / 50 ml	Double cream
1	Vanilla pod
3	Egg yolks
6¼ tbsp / 125 gm	Caster sugar

For the strawberry coulis:

200 gm	Strawberries, fresh

Method:

1. **For the sablé pastry,** whisk the sugar and egg yolks together until creamy. Add the baking powder, salt, and flour. Mix well. Add the butter and refrigerate for 2 hours.
2. Roll out the dough into ½" thickness. Cut into discs of 3" diameter. Bake in the oven for 10 minutes at 180°C / 390°F. Remove and keep aside to cool.
3. **For the crème brulée,** boil the milk and cream with the vanilla pod. Remove and cool.
4. Mix the egg yolks and sugar till the sugar dissolves. Pour over the cooked milk. Mix well. Bake at 170°C / 370°F. When cold, cut 2 discs of crème brulée the same size as the pastry.
6. **For the strawberry coulis,** blend 100 gm strawberries in a food processor till smooth.

Service:

Place a disc of crème brulée in the centre of a pastry. Arrange the strawberries on top of it and pour the coulis around.

WINE SUGGESTION: CHAMPAGNE OR DESSERT WINE

FRESH STRAWBERRY SORBET

Ingredients:

300 gm	Strawberries, very ripe or frozen strawberry purée	7 tbsp / 140 gm	Caster sugar
		4¼ tbsp / 85 ml	Water
		200 gm	Strawberries, fresh
½ tsp / 2½ ml	Lemon juice		

Method:

1. Purée the strawberries in a food processor (to extract 250 ml of purée).
2. Mix the strawberry purée with the lemon juice, sugar, and water until quite smooth. Churn and freeze until required.

Service:

Scoop the sorbet into glasses and decorate with fresh strawberries.

A ripe strawberry is a perfect love food, both innocent and sexy. The colour and shape tease the mind and excite the imagination. Try dipping them in chocolate, sour cream, and brown sugar or whipped cream!

WINE SUGGESTION: CHAMPAGNE OR SEMI-SWEET WHITE WINE

WINTER APRICOT TART TATIN

Ingredients:

36	Dry apricots, soaked for 1 hour	a pinch	Salt
		5 tbsp / 100 gm	Sugar
5 tbsp / 100 gm	Sugar	2 tsp	Butter
2 cups / 500 ml	Water	2 scoops	Apricot or vanilla ice cream
For the shortcrust pastry:			
1 cup / 125 gm	Refined flour	a few strands	Saffron
1 cup / 200 gm	Soft butter	2 sprigs	Mint
1	Egg		

Method:

1. Cook the sugar in a medium pot with 2 cups water; bring to the boil. Now add the drained apricots and cook for 30 minutes. Let it rest in the liquid for an hour, then drain.
2. **For the shortcrust pastry,** mix all the ingredients together. Knead the dough gently for 2 minutes and refrigerate for 2 hours.
3. Roll out the dough with a rolling pin and cut two discs of 3" diameter.
4. In a non-stick mould of 3" diameter, melt 1 tsp butter. Add 1 tbsp sugar and cook till the sugar is almost caramel colour. Repeat with the second mould.
5. Arrange the apricots inside each mould (12 each) and place a disc of the shortcrust pastry exactly the same size as the mould over it. Bake in the oven for 15 minutes.
6. **For the apricot sauce,** blend the remaining apricots in a food processor with 1 cup water. Mix well to obtain a fluid consistency.

This expensive spice has been reputed to work like a sex hormone and make erogenous zones even more sensitive. Saffron is made from the dried stigmas of a type of crocus.

WINE SUGGESTION: CHAMPAGNE OR SWEET WHITE WINE

Service:

When the tarts are cooked, turn them over onto a plate. Make sure the apricots are on top. Place a scoop of ice cream on top of each tart garnished with a few strands of saffron and mint sprigs.

Note: *The tarts can be made a couple of hours before dinner and be warmed up.*

Apricots are high in vitamin A and C, with a good amount of potassium. They belong to the rose family, no wonder when they are ripe, they smell great. There are as many as ten different varieties, but only two are majorly produced, Castlebrite and Patterson. Apricots colour range from yellow to a golden orange with a red blush.

TOWER OF CARAMEL TOFFEE AND GINGER LEMON APPLE CREAM

Ingredients:

For the toffee:

100 gm	Almonds
1 cup / 250 ml	Water
1 cup / 250 gm	Sugar

For the ginger lemon apple cream:

3	Juice of lemons
3	Lemon rind
1 tbsp / 18 gm	Ginger, grated
2	Eggs
1 cup / 250 gm	Sugar

¹/₂ cup / 175 gm	Apple purée, cooked
1¹/₂ cups / 425 ml	Cream, whipped

For the pistachio sauce:

¹/₂ cup / 60 gm	Pistachios, peeled, chopped
4¹/₂ tbsp / 90 gm	Sugar
2	Egg yolks
3 cups / 750 ml	Milk, boiled

Pistachios or any other nuts have had a reputation as aphrodisiacs for centuries. During harvest festivals in Rome, maidens passed out bowls of nuts as symbols of fertility.

Method:

1. Caramalize water and sugar; add almonds. Remove from heat, pour the caramel on greaseproof paper and cool. On hardening break into small pieces and blend to obtain a fine powder.
2. Spread this powder on a round 3" baking tray, lined with greaseproof paper and bake at 150°C / 330°F for 2 minutes.
3. **For the ginger lemon apple cream,** mix all the ingredients (except the cream) and bring to a simmer. Remove from heat before it comes to the boil. Keep aside to cool. When cold, add the cream.
4. **For the pistachio sauce,** whisk sugar and yolks until they whiten. Add milk and pistachios; cook for 2 minutes without boiling.

Service:

Spread the ginger lemon apple cream on the toffee circles and layer it 3-4 times on the plate. Top with a toffee disc. Pour pistachio sauce around the plate and garnish with fresh mint.

(See p. 76 for picture)

Native to China, peaches have long been associated with ripe sexuality by the Chinese. The best peaches have a wonderful aroma and give in to slight pressure.

FRESH PEACH SOUP WITH CHAMPAGNE AND EXOTIC FRUIT PEARLS

Ingredients:

1 kg	Peaches	4	Strawberries,
1 cup / 250 ml	Champagne		diced
100 gm	Watermelon,	100 gm	Melon, diced
	diced	100 gm	Papaya, diced
2	Kiwis, diced	2 sprigs	Mint

Method:

1. Cook peaches in boiling water for 2 minutes to peel off the skin.
2. Stone the peaches and purée the flesh in a food processor.
3. Mix at a very high speed with champagne for 2-3 minutes. Add 1-2 tsp fine sugar, if needed. Refrigerate for 3 hours.

Service:

Pour the cold peach soup into a soup plate and garnish with watermelon, kiwis, strawberries, melon, and papaya. Add a mint sprig.

Note: *This dessert has to be eaten very cold to be thoroughly enjoyed. It can be prepared several hours before dinner.*

With their glowing, smoldering crimson or scarlet skins and high gloss, cherries seem too good to be true. Cherries contain an highly toxic chemical which appears to have a stimulating effect on the sexual organs, especially in men.

CHERRY CLAFOUTI

Ingredients:

100 gm	Cherries, depitted	10 tbsp / 200 gm	Icing sugar
4 tbsp / 40 gm	Refined flour	1	Egg
2 tbsp / 40 gm	Sugar	a pinch	Salt
a pinch	Salt	¾ cup / 90 gm	Refined flour
2 tsp / 10 ml	Milk	**For the sauce:**	
1	Egg	¾ cup / 200 gm	Sugar
For the shortcrust pastry:		100 gm	Cherries, depitted
2½ tbsp / 50 gm	Butter		

Method:

1. **For the shortcrust pastry,** whip the butter and icing sugar until fluffy. Add the egg and salt. Fold in the flour and refrigerate for 2 hours.
2. Roll out the dough and cut 2 discs each (4" diameter and 3 mm thick). Lay the discs in moulds with 3" diameter and ½" height. Bake the pastry in the oven at 200°C / 430°F for 6 minutes.
3. Mix the flour, sugar, and salt in a bowl. Pour the milk gently and add the egg. Then add the cherries. Pour the mixture in the moulds and bake for 20 minutes at 210°C / 450°F.
4. **For the sauce,** mix the sugar in 200 ml boiling water.
5. Blend the cherries in a high speed blender and then add the sugar syrup to thin the sauce.

Service:

Place 1 tart on each plate and pour the sauce around. Eat warm.

Index